Joyfully Married

A 30-day creative love,
relationship growth, and
happy marriage challenge

Jed Jurchenko

www.CoffeeShopConversations.com

© 2020 by Jed Jurchenko.

A thirty-day challenge to inspire you and your loved one to connect more often, more deeply, and more joyfully than ever before!

Also by Jed

131 Creative Conversations for Couples

131 Engaging Conversations for Couples

131 Creative Conversations for Families

131 Necessary Conversations before Marriage

131 Conversations that Engage Kids

131 Conversations for Stepfamily Success

131 Boredom Busters and Creativity Builders

131 Stress Busters and Mood Boosters for Kids

Coffee Shop Conversations Psychology
and the Bible: Live, Love, and Lead Well

Coffee Shop Inspirations: Simple Strategies for
Building Dynamic Leadership and Relationships

Bonus Gifts

To thank you for your purchase, I would like to send you two bonus gifts. First, get a free copy of my eBook *131 Holiday Conversations*!

Then, dive into the *Joyfully Married* group experience! Here, you'll find more resources for breaking out of the average by connecting with your loved one more deeply, more often, and more joyfully than ever before!

Get the bonuses here:
www.coffeeshopconversations.com/joyfullymarried

Dedication

To, Jenny, my amazing wife:

I am blessed to have you in my life and am
incredibly grateful for our many wonderful moments
of connection on this wild ride. I wouldn't have
things any other way.
I love you like crazy!

Table of Contents

Table of Contents

Breaking Out
of the Average

Schools teach math, history, and science, but provide little instruction on how to do relationships well. Since few couples pursue this knowledge on their own, it's not surprising the divorce rate is roughly 50 percent.

A favorite college professor once said, "Some couples put more effort into researching their next vehicle purchase than in getting to know their spouse." After nearly two decades of working with couples and families, I'm afraid he's right. For some reason, it's assumed couples will know how to connect.

Sadly, in marriage, the odds are not in our favor. Out of the unions that last, far too many couples are stuck in a bland limbo. They exist somewhere between saying, "I do" on their wedding day and finding happily ever after. Others white-knuckle it, remaining together by sheer grit alone. These couples fall asleep, back to back, each night, wondering, *When will the pain end?*

In marriage, being average is not good enough. Fortunately, you are not average! I know because you are reading this book. Nineteenth-century pastor Peter Marshall called wedlock "the highest halls of human happiness." And every good fairy tale reminds us that couples are supposed to ride into the sunset—delighting in love for the rest of their days. Despite the dreary statistics, a marvelous union is still possible.

Couples can bridge the gap between where they are and where they want to be, and more support is available than ever before. In the past, love was primarily an art. Those with happy marriages offered their best relationship advice, but their wisdom was based primarily on assumptions.

Today our understanding of relationships has grown. The science is now so precise that relationship expert John Gottman can predict with an astounding 91 percent accuracy whether a marriage will succeed or fail after observing a couple for only five minutes.[1]

Thanks to fMRI scans, we now know the impact our closest bond has on the human brain—and the results are astounding! A caring connection to our spouse

- makes life's bright moments brighter.
- keeps us healthier. This includes reducing the risk of mental illnesses and heart attacks.
- causes life's difficult moments—both physically and emotionally painful—to hurt less.

Science has confirmed what fairy tales have told us all along. Married couples can, indeed, be among the happiest people on earth. Thanks to the latest research, we now know why some relationships brilliantly succeed while others fail.

For couples who long to take their bond to the next level, this is excellent news.

Regardless of the current state of your marriage, immense growth is possible. In fact, I believe your future is so bright, the two of you may need to wear shades!

The Missing Piece

Growing up, my siblings and I loved putting puzzles together. As the oldest child, I took pride in placing the last piece. As my brother and sister grew, the three of us raced to the finish. Fearing that one day I would lose this competition, I devised a plan.

I would hide a single piece in my pocket when there were still too many pieces on the table to notice one missing. When only this piece remained, I would drop to the floor and pretend to look for it. Once my siblings joined the search, I casually stood up, finished the puzzle, and smugly walked away. Yes, this was sneaky, I know.

In marriage, there is also a missing piece. That piece is action. Although gaining new insights is important, most couples could significantly improve their relationship by simply applying what they already know. Because applying new knowledge can be difficult, this book keeps things simple with a daily action challenge.

Science and Action

Science and action are a dynamic duo with the power to lift your relationship to the next level. To help you apply each principle, this book is divided into thirty chapters. Every reading begins with a teaching—which is the easy part. Some chapters will contain "ah-ha moments," while others will remind you of the invaluable wisdom you already possess.

Next comes the crucial part—the challenge. This is where genuine transformation occurs. The challenges make this book unique because they provide specific steps for growth. If you and your spouse take one small step to improve your marriage each day for the next thirty days, just imagine how much your relationship will grow!

Let's expand on this idea. You might view this book as a way of applying the domino effect to your marriage. Here's what I mean. In 1983, Lorne Whitehead published an article in *The American Journal of Physics* entitled "Domino 'chain reaction.'"[2] Lorne discovered that each domino in a series can knock down a block approximately one-and-a-half times larger than itself. This means a two-inch domino can push over a three-inch domino, which can knock down a four-and-a-half-inch domino.

According to Lorne's research, if this pattern continues, domino number thirty-two will be large enough to topple a skyscraper. Now that is some exponential growth. By developing your bond daily, small changes compound. Like Lorne's chain of dominos, you and your loved one can also experience immense growth!

What Happy Couples Know

If there is one secret happy couples know — or in *Lord of the Rings* language, "One ring to rule them all," — it is summed up in this sentence: In marriage, a caring connection matters most. This probably isn't a surprise. When I ask couples how they know they are in love, they typically answer as follows:

- We put each other's needs first.
- We give each other our undivided attention.
- We are honest with one another.
- The two of us talk about everything.
- We can't wait to spend time together.

A common theme in these answers is the couple's caring connection that takes precedence over all else. Couples fall in love because they enjoy spending time together, and they stay in love because they are thrilled to be in one another's presence. Anything beyond this — including exquisite dates, excellent communication, or similar interests — is merely icing on the cake.

As we will see, a caring connection is more than a nicety; it's a necessity — one the human brain puts on par with oxygen. This book will guide you in infusing the life-giving oxygen of connection into your relationship. So, get ready to gain new insights. But even more importantly, prepare to act.

Although average couples live in quiet desperation, you and your spouse can break out of the ordinary and be joyfully married. So, brew a cup of coffee, tea, or grab another favorite beverage. Then dive into this relationship adventure. I wish you happy reading and happy connecting!

Day 1:
The Moment We Met

Jenny and I connected through an online dating site, and we met at a tiny pizzeria with a breathtaking view of San Diego Bay. When I first saw Jenny, I thought to myself, *Wow, she is gorgeous!* From there, things got even better.

Over dinner, I was captivated by Jenny's soft smile and her genuine compassion for others. But it was during a sunset walk along the shore, that Jenny impressed me the most. As the two of us strolled side-by-side, I noticed a snafu I thought would end our perfect evening, and my heart sank.

After the sun went down, the night air cooled quickly. It was mid-February, and I hadn't asked Jenny to bring a jacket. When I saw Jenny shiver, I asked "It's cold out. Do you want to turn back?" Much to my delight, she sweetly replied, "No, I'm fine."

A few minutes later, Jenny had goosebumps running up and down her arms. I asked a second time if she wanted to turn around, and Jenny again sweetly declined. But as our walk progressed, Jenny's shivering increased. It was obvious she was cold.

Wanting to be polite, I suggested we turn around a third time. This time Jenny responded with a firm determination: "No, I'm fine. Let's keep going." After our date, I couldn't stop thinking about this amazing woman who wanted to be with me more than she wanted to warm up.

So, what did I do next? I made Jenny wait an entire two weeks before calling again. Yes, this actually happened! I thought to myself, *If Jenny and I go out a second time, there is a good chance we'll fall in love and get married.* I wasn't sure I was ready for this.

Fortunately, Jenny is patient. Two long weeks passed before I made up my mind. When I asked Jenny out a second time, she said, "Yes!" Twenty-one months later, I proposed, and we married a year after that. Now, here we are — with six kids and seven incredible years into our marriage. This is our love story in a nutshell. What's yours?

Celebrating Connection Moments

Studies show that emotional connection is the foundation of a joy-filled relationship. Much value is found in reminiscing over the happy times. In *The Joyfully Connected Challenge*, celebrate the highpoints of when you and your loved one first met.

This challenge contains a separate page for each of you, but you might want to talk through your answers too. There is not a single right way to complete this challenge. As long as you and your loved one are drawing close, you are doing things right!

The Joyfully Connected Challenge
for Her

When I first laid eyes on my spouse, I thought to myself_____

_____

_____

_____

_____

An especially memorable moment from our first date happened when _____

_____

_____

_____

A quality I admired in him when we first met was _____

_____

_____

_____

A quality I greatly admire in him today is

_____

_____

_____

The Joyfully Connected Challenge
for Him

When I first laid eyes on my spouse, I thought to myself _____

_____

_____

_____

_____

An especially memorable moment from our first date happened when _____

_____

_____

_____

A quality I admired in her when we first met was _____

_____

_____

_____

A quality I greatly admire in her today is

_____

_____

_____

Day 2:
Building Momentum with Gratitude

For nearly a decade, I worked closely with hurting parents. Some were jobless. Others were trying to regain custody of their kids. All of them had few supports.

As a paid professional, I was supposed to make a difference — which felt like a daunting task. Then I discovered a simple question with the power to renew energy and restore joy. After a brief introduction, I would ask a family, "Now that we've met, tell me, what's going good in your life?"

This inquiry was always met with surprise. A period of drawn-out silence would be followed by a single word — "Nothing." But I am persistent and a firm believer that there is always something going right in everybody's life. The trick is finding it.

I challenged families to work together to list ten positives—no matter how small. This process always started slow. But as family members identified tiny blessings in their lives, momentum built up fast. By the time families reached ten positives, the entire atmosphere in the room lifted.

Minutes earlier, the air felt thick and heavy. Now there was energy, excitement, and hope for a brighter future. What I learned from these experiences is that gratitude changes us.

An attitude of appreciation may come easily, or it might be a challenge. Either way, right now is an excellent time to break free from any lingering negativity and build momentum. Do this by focusing on the good things in your lives.

"What's going good?" remains one of my favorite questions to this day. Perhaps you and your spouse are stuck in a negative tunnel vision. Maybe the two of you are facing a daunting challenge or could use an added energy boost. Whether your relationship is currently surviving or thriving, focusing on all that is right in the world is an excellent way to increase marital joy.

In *The Momentum Challenge*, share five things you are thankful for right now. If you get stuck, ask your loved one for help. For bonus points, increase your list to ten. After completing this challenge, find a way to celebrate the many blessings you have!

The Momentum Challenge for Her

Good things are always happening. The trick is finding them. Complete this challenge by listing five positives. Give yourself bonus points for filling in all ten blanks.

Some good things in my life include:

1. _____

2. _____

3. _____

4. _____

5. _____

6. _____

7. _____

8. _____

9. _____

10. _____

The Momentum Challenge for Him

Good things are always happening. The trick is finding them. Complete this challenge by listing five positives. Give yourself bonus points for filling in all ten blanks.

Some good things in my life include:

1. _____

2. _____

3. _____

4. _____

5. _____

6. _____

7. _____

8. _____

9. _____

10. _____

Day 3:
Updating Love Maps

Jenny has a hidden adventurous side. When we started dating, she shared that her secret ambition is to swim with great white sharks. If you ever watched *The Nature Channel* and saw a woman enter a metal cage in shark-infested waters, then you know what Jenny aspires to do.

A few weeks after discovering this, I took Jenny on a date to La Jolla Shores, where we snorkeled with leopard sharks. Leopard sharks eat clams, crabs, and shrimp — not humans — so they are safe to swim with. Because they grow nearly five feet long, it's still quite the adventure.

As the two of us ventured into the sea, in our wetsuits, snorkels, and masks, I took Jenny's hand in mine. Leopard sharks soon surrounded us. When a shark passed just out of arm's reach, I let go of Jenny's hand, dove in pursuit, and gently stroked its back. This was a mistake!

When I resurfaced, Jenny jumped into my arms, sputtering. "Please don't do that again!" I was stunned to learn this amazing woman, who is eager to swim with great white sharks, was terrified the moment I left her side. Nevertheless, Jenny's passion for swimming with sharks continued to grow. This adventure even made it onto our first dream board. I, of course, promised to be the supportive husband cheering Jenny on from inside the boat.

Swimming with great whites is an adventure that hasn't happened yet. With our family of six kids, I assumed this desire was outdated, but I wanted to be sure. On a recent date, I asked Jenny, "Honey, that old dream of cage diving with sharks, you don't still want to do that, do you?" Much to my surprise, Jenny replied, "Of course I do! I don't talk about it often because our family has other priorities."

This story illustrates the value of updating our love maps. According to John Gottman, we all carry internal love maps or mental images of our spouse in our minds. These love maps form early in our relationship when we ask about best friends, favorite foods, hopes, dreams, fears, and aspirations.

As time passes, we may assume our loved one hasn't changed and begin operating from an outdated love map. In my case, I wrongly assumed Jenny's aspiration had changed. According to Gottman, updated love maps are essential because "emotionally intelligent couples are intimately familiar with each other's world." They have "richly detailed love maps."[3]

This means ongoing curiosity is a must. Your spouse isn't the same as when you first met. If it has been a year or more since you updated your love maps, then you may be in for a surprise.

The Love Map Challenge will assist you in updating your internal love maps. This challenge comes in the form of a quiz for added fun. First, record how you think your loved one will answer. Then see if you are right.

The Love Map Challenge for Her

1. My spouse's best friend is _____

2. My spouse's favorite meal is _____

3. If my spouse had a day off, he would want to relax by _____

4. The type of movies my spouse enjoys most are (comedies, action, love stories, etc.)
_____

5. A current worry my loved one has is
_____

6. Some of my spouse's life dreams include
_____

7. My spouse feels especially loved when I
_____

8. My spouse's favorite activity that we do together is _____

9. On a scale of one to ten, how energized is your spouse by his job? A one means "it's draining" and ten signifies "it's incredibly energizing." _____

10. My loved one would most like to travel to
_____

The Love Map Challenge for Him

1. My spouse's best friend is _____

2. My spouse's favorite meal is _____

3. If my spouse had a day off, she would want to relax by _____

4. The type of movies my spouse enjoys most are (comedies, action, love stories, etc.)
   _____

5. A current worry my loved one has is
   _____

6. Some of my spouse's life dreams include
   _____

7. My spouse feels especially loved when I
   _____

8. My spouse's favorite activity to do together is _____

9. On a scale of one to ten, how energized is your spouse by her job? A one means "it's draining" and ten signifies "it's incredibly energizing." _____

10. My loved one would most like to travel to
    _____

Day 4:
Growing in Intimacy

My favorite definition of intimacy is "into-me-see." Intimacy involves seeing into our loved one's inner world. It means knowing our loved ones and being fully known by them. Intimacy can be scary because sharing mistakes, desires, hopes, and fears requires vulnerability. Yet in safe relationships, there is enormous value in allowing our self to be known. I even have a favorite metaphor to illustrate this.

Years ago, I worked at a church. After purchasing my first condo, kind families donated their used cookware so I could get off to a good start. Many generous families were eager to help, and I accumulated an abundance of pans. The excess was helpful because I was new to cooking and burned food often.

Sometimes meals were so badly charred that I tossed the entire pan in the trash—yes, it was that bad! Then I discovered the joy of nonstick pans. No matter how messy my cooking became, the pan was easily cleaned. The timing couldn't have been better because I was nearly out of pans.

Although a smooth, nonstick coating is wonderful on pans, it's far less desirable on human beings. Acting composed all of the time hinders genuine connection because flaws, rough edges, and humanness are what allow relationships to stick. In other words, imperfect people connect best with other imperfect people.

This principle took me over a decade to learn. I used to shy away from sharing that our family is blended. After all, I am not proud of having a failed marriage in my past. I thought, *My life is messy, so there is no way I can help others.* Fortunately, today I know better.

Jenny remarked on numerous occasions that our blended family caused the two of us to work together fast. More difficulties led to increased teamwork and quick growth. Past problems have also opened the doors for connecting with other hurting couples and allow us to relate with their pain.

A little-known fact about me is that our family consists of two biological children, two stepchildren, and two foster children. We are twice blended. Today, I'm a firm believer that God loves blended families, and we wouldn't have our family any other way. This little-known fact is one I am working to share more openly.

In *The Into-me-see Challenge*, share something about you that your loved one doesn't know. The revelation can be big or small, as long as you divulge your inner world. If you get stuck, use one of the prompts below to get started.

1. A current fear is…
2. Something I'm secretly excited about is…

3. A time I was especially grateful for you and haven't told you about happened when…

4. A worry that keeps me up at night is…

5. One of my dreams that sounds too big to share is…

6. A recent interest I haven't told you about is…

7. A recent event that made me sad is…

The Into-me-see Challenge for Her

Complete *The Into-me-see Challenge* by revealing something your loved one doesn't know. This can be a fact about you, a current feeling, a future dream, or a creative idea you haven't shared yet.

_____

_____

_____

_____

_____

_____

_____

_____

_____

_____

_____

_____

_____

_____

_____

_____

_____

_____

The Into-me-see Challenge for Him

Complete *The Into-me-see Challenge* by revealing something your loved one doesn't know. This can be a fact about you, a current feeling, a future dream, or a creative idea you haven't shared yet.

_____

_____

_____

_____

_____

_____

_____

_____

_____

_____

_____

_____

_____

_____

_____

_____

Day 5:
Closing Loops

I once heard a pastor share an ingenious strategy he uses to reduce conflict in his marriage. This pastor would routinely connect with parishioners by phone as he drove home. But a problem arose the moment he walked through the door. His wife and kids were waiting to connect and clamored for his attention. Of course, the person on the other end of the call also wanted to finish the conversation.

Tensions grew, and this pastor knew something needed to change. So, he created a simple rule. This wise pastor decided he would end all calls before stepping out of the car. This way, he could give his wife and children his undivided attention.

This story illustrates the power of closing loops. Contrary to popular belief, attention is finite. We have a limited amount to give.

Many people wander through life with countless tasks on their to-do list. There are bills to pay, emails to answer, and daily chores that must get done. Like a computer with hundreds of browser windows open, many people have little memory to spare. If this pattern continues, they will eventually crash.

An abundance of open loops also makes focusing on our loved one difficult. The purpose of closing loops is to free up mental energy for the ones who matter most. How are you at fully engaging with your spouse? Can you focus on what he or she says, or does your mind wander from one activity to the next?

If you have difficulty giving your spouse your undivided attention, then closing loops is for you. First, make a list of all the open loops in your life. Then set aside a few hours to close as many as possible. Start with the most manageable tasks first. You don't need to accomplish everything, just free up enough mental space to fully attend to your loved one. If you have ever been deeply listened to, in a way that can almost be felt, then you know the power of giving someone your full attention.

In *The Loop-closing Challenge*, identify ten open loops and close them fast. Free up mental space so you can give your loved one the present of your full presence!

The Loop-closing Challenge for Her

Complete today's challenge by listing ten loops you will close fast. Check the box to the right once each task is complete.

1. _____ ☐

2. _____ ☐

3. _____ ☐

4. _____ ☐

5. _____ ☐

6. _____ ☐

7. _____ ☐

8. _____ ☐

9. _____ ☐

10. _____ ☐

Now that more mental space is available, when will you give your spouse your undivided attention?

_____

_____

_____

The Loop-closing Challenge for Him

Complete today's challenge by listing ten loops you will close fast. Check the box to the right once each task is complete.

1. _____ ☐
2. _____ ☐
3. _____ ☐
4. _____ ☐
5. _____ ☐
6. _____ ☐
7. _____ ☐
8. _____ ☐
9. _____ ☐
10. _____ ☐

Now that more mental space is available, when will you give your spouse your undivided attention?

_____
_____
_____

Day 6:
Celebrating Differences

A friend once shared how he almost planned a romantic date for his wife. He envisioned a candlelight dinner, soft music, and a rose-petal path leading to their bedroom. This man nearly followed through with his plan until he envisioned his wife opening the door. He realized his wife's first thought would be, *Who is going to clean up this mess?*

So instead, my friend took his wife to an elegant restaurant, and afterward they explored the town. This was a date his wife truly enjoyed! I love this story because it reminds me that Jenny and I have different tastes, and this is a good thing. If we were both the same, then one of us wouldn't be needed. Plus, Jenny's unique interests add value to my life.

Jenny's passion for family trips is one way she stretches me for the better. I am more of a homebody, and these excursions push me outside of my comfort zone. Yet at the end of the year, I always see them as highpoints.

In marriage, differences are worth celebrating. So, which statement describes your ideal Friday night, and which would your loved one choose? Do you know?

1. A night on the town
2. Dinner at a fancy restaurant
3. A movie and popcorn
4. A night at home, with an early bedtime

There are no right or wrong answers. The key is knowing where the two of you are alike, where you differ, and celebrating both. Common interests make connecting easy, while differences create the opportunity for growth.

Because of Jenny, I think differently than I did a decade ago. I'm kinder, more compassionate, and I plan better. Hopefully, Jenny is better off because of my unique tastes too. The ways you and your loved one differ can be a catalyst for growth. In *The Differences Challenge,* express appreciation for your partner's unique interests which add value to your life.

The Differences Challenge for Her

Complete this challenge by listing four ways you and your loved one differ.

1. _____
2. _____
3. _____
4. _____

Then write your loved one a note. Describe how his unique tastes add value to your life.

_____
_____
_____
_____
_____
_____
_____
_____
_____
_____
_____
_____
_____

The Differences Challenge for Him

Complete this challenge by listing four ways you and your loved one differ.

1. _____
2. _____
3. _____

Then write your loved one a note. Describe how her unique tastes add value to your life.

_____
_____
_____
_____
_____
_____
_____
_____
_____
_____
_____
_____

Day 7:
Reminiscing with Joy

Reminiscing isn't just small talk. Studies show that couples with close emotional bonds have happier, longer-lasting relationships. Focusing on happy times is a lot like glue; it binds a couple together.

Our human brains are always at work. Therapists use the word *self-talk* to describe the internal dialogue that continually plays in our heads. For most people, this head talk is bent toward the negative. We awfulize and catastrophize, building up events to be far worse than they are. Or we focus on past hurts and grow increasingly bitter.

Fortunately, we don't have to allow our negative chatterbox to steal the show. We can reminisce about the happy times instead. Our internal chatterbox is going to talk away, because that is what chatterboxes do. The good news is that we can steer the conversation.

Here is an example of what steering a mental conversation looks like. Before Jenny and I married, one of our favorite adventures was a trip to Catalina Island. The day was filled with paragliding, lunch on the beach, a trip to the arcade—where we played copious amounts of ski-ball—and exploring the island. Amid the fun, it was the time with Jenny that mattered most. This is how I knew I was falling in love.

Days like this one are what I want my internal voice to dwell upon. If our inner chatterboxes must talk, then let's give them something worth talking about. In *The Reminiscing Challenge*, reflect on an amazing moment together. Remind your chatterbox of a time so remarkable you would relive it if you could.

The Reminiscing Challenge for Her

Complete this challenge by reflecting on a time with your spouse that was so amazing you would relive it if you could.

_____

_____

_____

_____

_____

_____

_____

_____

_____

_____

_____

_____

_____

_____

_____

_____

_____

_____

_____

The Reminiscing Challenge for Him

Complete this challenge by reflecting on a time with your spouse that was so amazing you would relive it if you could.

_____

_____

_____

_____

_____

_____

_____

_____

_____

_____

_____

_____

_____

_____

_____

_____

_____

_____

_____

_____

_____

Day 8:
Our Bucket List

Amazing things happen when couples dream big. A few years ago, Jenny and I were encouraged to build a dream board—which is essentially a bucket list with pictures. To construct our dream board, we gathered a poster board, glue, and our laptops. Then we met at the dining room table to brainstorm.

Each time we agreed on an aspiration, we scoured the internet for a visual representation. We printed these pictures, cut them out, added them to our dream board, and hung it in our office.

Psychology tells us the human mind is always at work—both consciously and subconsciously. The dream board's purpose is to focus the subconscious mind and keep us moving toward our goals. Over time, our dream board made its way from our office to a wall in our garage. Eventually, Jenny and I stopped noticing it and assumed we did the exercise wrong.

However, two years later, something astounding happened. As I removed our tattered dream board from the wall, I noticed an image of a house — smack-dab in the middle. Scrawled underneath were the words, "We will purchase a home."

I enthusiastically brought the board to Jenny. When we created our dream board, the thought of owning a home seemed impossible, but we dreamed big anyway. Two years later, we found ourselves packing to move into the house we just purchased.

As we talked through the other images, Jenny and I were astounded at how many dreams came to fruition. So, does our subconscious mind really strive to make our dreams a reality? Jenny and I aren't sure. We both thank God whole-heartedly, believing He had much to do with this. In addition, we continue to update our dream board yearly — which once again hangs in our office.

When Jenny and I reflected on our dreams this year, we were again impressed at how many have become a reality. Sometimes these dreams happen in scary and unexpected ways—yet they still happen! One of my all-time favorite quotes is from Bill Gates, who said, "Most people overestimate what they can do in one year and underestimate what they can do in ten years." Jenny and I know this is true. We discovered the value of dreaming big, scary dreams together.

Whether you and your loved one create a dream board, a bucket list, or ten-year goals, the most important things are to dream big, dream often, and to write your dreams down. In *The Bucket List Challenge,* work together to create your bucket list.

For bonus points, turn your list into a dream board. Start by printing a visual representation for each dream. Then cut your images out, glue them to your board, and hang it in a place you will see it often. Use the challenge on the next page to get started.

The Bucket List Challenge

Complete this challenge by starting a couple's bucket list. For bonus points, transform your list into a dream board.

1. _____

2. _____

3. _____

4. _____

5. _____

6. _____

7. _____

8. _____

9. _____

10. _____

11. _____

12. _____

Day 9:
Breaking Out of Busy

I can't believe how busy I am! In my early twenties, I thought this often. Now I realize that I had no idea what *busy* actually meant. Sure, I was going to school, had errands to run, and work to do. But when I said, "I'm busy," what I actually meant was

- I'm not sure how I'm going to find time to watch all the movies I want to see.
- I can't possibly mountain bike, read, and spend time with friends on the same day.
- There are so many adventures to be had, and the day isn't long enough for all of them.

Busyness meant video games, talking on the phone, hiking, and ample time with friends. Now, as a daddy to six kiddos, *busy* has new meaning. It entails:

- working overtime
- folding infinite piles of laundry
- completing household chores
- bussing the children from one activity to the next
- paying bills
- racing to keep up with life

Although I'm a huge believer in the value of hard work, I also know that bouncing from one activity to the next, like a flea who guzzled the latest energy drink, will not do. Busy is the archenemy of relationships because it keeps us from connecting with the ones who matter most.

In marriage, busyness is the new smoking. It's an addictive habit that is hazardous to our interpersonal health. Like smoking, being busy has become a status symbol, and the phrase *I'm busy* is the trendy answer to the question, *How are you?*

Don't let busyness suffocate your relationship. Kick the hustle and bustle habit instead. Advantages of breaking out of busy include, more time for:

- family fun
- dates with your spouse
- books you enjoy
- sleep
- space for spontaneous adventure

If the thought of slowing down is exhilarating, know that accomplishing this is no easy feat. I can personally attest to the addictive nature of busyness. Like many people, my biggest timewaster is my smartphone. Phone time is deceptive because it feels like work but accomplishes little. My goal is to be more intentional about separating work time from family time, as there is no benefit to combining the two. I share this because you and I are on this journey together.

One family I know places a smartphone basket by their door. This is where the cellphones reside when the workday is over.

Whether you employ a similar strategy or have your own ideas, the important thing is to take action. Living like a bad amateur plate spinner, frantically trying to keep up, may be required for a season but is not a viable plan for long-term success.

Because a caring connection is the foundation of a joyful marriage, reducing busyness is a must. So, what's your chief time waster? And do you have a plan for kicking this habit? In *The Break-Out-of-Busy Challenge*, take steps to breaking free from life's hustle and bustle so you can connect with your loved one.

The Break-Out-of-Busy
Challenge for Her

Complete today's challenge by reducing busyness. Then, connect with your spouse more often, more deeply, and more joyfully than ever before.

If I was less busy, my loved one and I would have more time to _____

_____

_____

_____

My biggest time waster is _____

A new strategy for breaking out of busy that I plan to try is _____

_____

_____   _____

I will intentionally slow down and connect with my loved one today by _____

_____

_____

_____

The Break-Out-of-Busy
Challenge for Him

Complete today's challenge by reducing busyness. Then, connect with your spouse more often, more deeply, and more joyfully than ever before.

If I was less busy, my loved one and I would have more time to _____

_____

_____

_____

My biggest time waster is _____

A new strategy for breaking out of busy that I plan to try is _____

_____

_____

I will intentionally slow down and connect with my loved one today by _____

_____

_____

_____

Day 10:
Creative Love

I especially enjoy acts of creative love. Over the years, I've compiled a list of my favorite exploits. One of the best ideas comes from a comedian who wrote, "I love you," on every egg in the carton. Then there is the story of the Navy Seal who hid notes around the house before each deployment. His wife cherished finding them one by one.

Finally, in *Nightlife*, a devotional for couples, Dr. James Dobson describes how his grandparents wrote "SHMILY" everywhere. The acronym stands for "See how much I love you." The couple scrawled this on notes, the fogged bathroom mirror, and anyplace they could find. This ingenious idea turned their love into a game.

As a fan of creative love, I also have my own story to tell. After hearing about Jenny's appreciation for whales, I drove to an eclectic gift shop to buy a stuffed whale in a can.

When I presented her with this gift, I even included a can opener. Watching Jenny's confused look turn to delight after she opened the can was fun to watch, and the gift was so meaningful that she still has it a decade later.

The point is that love can and should be fun. If the two of you are not finding ample reasons for joy, then you might be doing love wrong. Contrary to popular belief, enjoyment is much more than fluff. Fun is so essential the renowned therapist William Glasser includes it on his list of basic human needs. As you may have guessed, creativity and fun are intertwined. Albert Einstein even proclaimed, "Creativity is intelligence having fun."

Finding creative ways to make your marriage a blast can be as simple as

- hiding love notes around the house
- giving a unique gift
- telling a joke
- sending humorous cards
- playing a goofy game together

- Finding reasons to laugh amid stressors and chaos

How are you and your spouse putting creativity to work? In *The Creative-love Challenge,* exert your imagination and increase the joy in your bond.

The Creative-Love Challenge for Her

Complete *The Creative-Love Challenge* by filling in the prompts below and then performing an act of creative love.

Dear husband, thank you for loving me in creative ways. An act of creative love that was especially meaningful happened when you

_____

_____

_____

_____

_____

_____

I'm excited about getting creative together. Something new I am eager to try is _____

_____

_____

_____

_____

I creatively expressed love to my spouse by

_____

_____

The Creative-Love Challenge for Him

Complete *The Creative-Love Challenge* by filling in the prompts below and then performing an act of creative love.

Dear wife, thank you for loving me in creative ways. An act of creative love that was especially meaningful happened when you

_____

_____

_____

_____

_____

_____

I'm excited about getting creative together. Something new I can't wait to try is _____

_____

_____

_____

_____

I creatively expressed love to my spouse by

_____

_____

Day 11:
Energize Your Bond

How do you view your relationship? Is love a duty, or is it celebrated? This question is more complex than it sounds, so don't answer too fast. While the words "Our marriage is a celebration" are fun to say, we often follow this with contradictory thoughts like *I have to connect with my loved one,* or *The two of us should go on a date.*

This is known as *stinking thinking,* and it drains energy from relationships. Other examples of stinking thinking include:

- I have to go to work.
- I should do chores.
- I must get this project done.
- I need to spend time with my spouse.

Thoughts that include the words *have to, need to, should,* and *must* add undue pressure and take the focus off of our options. In marriage, a stinking thinking mindset makes connecting with our loved one feel like a chore. These kinds of thoughts are also not in alignment with reality. As adults, there are few things we have to do. Yet many people get trapped in stinking thinking anyway.

A quick way to energize your relationship is to make a mental pivot. In the game of basketball, when a player is not allowed to dribble the ball, he can still pivot. A pivot lets the ball-handler change direction by moving one foot. This tiny shift helps him find open teammates and provides a broader view of the court.

A mental pivot is similar. It's a tiny shift in perspective that expands our joy. Here is what a mental pivot looks like:

- I work because I believe in what I do. I also like my coworkers, and the paycheck is nice too.

- Even though household tasks are not my favorite, I want to do chores because I enjoy a clean home.
- I spend time with my spouse because she is amazing. We don't date because "I have to" or because "we should spend time together." I date my wife because I genuinely enjoy being with her.

The mental pivot from *I have to* to *I want to* or, better yet, *I get to* quenches the stinking thinking mindset. Each morning, our thoughts set the tone for the day. Instead of telling yourself, *I have to…*, declare,

- I get to work.
- I can't wait to spend time with my spouse.
- And yes, I even want to do chores.

In *The Energizing Challenge*, rejuvenate your relationship by shifting from *I have to* to *I get to*.

The Energizing Challenge for Her

Complete today's challenge by filling in the blanks below.

As an adult, there are few things you must do. Write down five things you get to do today.

1. _____
2. _____
3. _____
4. _____
5. _____

Now, energize your relationship by listing five things you get to do with your loved one.

1. _____
2. _____
3. _____
4. _____
5. _____

The Energizing Challenge for Him

Complete today's challenge by filling in the blanks below.

As an adult, there are few things you must do. Write down five things you get to do today.

1. _____

2. _____

3. _____

4. _____

5. _____

Now, energize your relationship by listing five things you get to do with your loved one.

1. _____

2. _____

3. _____

4. _____

5. _____

Day 12:
Making the Most
of Chores

"People have to know themselves to lead themselves." My friends Scott and Michelle say these words often. Although this quote is usually applied to leadership, this statement also rings true in marriage. Couples work together more effectively when partners know themselves well.

When I ask couples, "What are your most significant barriers to joy?" the answer *household chores* is common. The problem with chores is that most people don't enjoy them, yet they must be done. This is where it helps to know our self and our loved one.

One of my responsibilities is taking out the trash. Why? I'm on garbage duty because Jenny despises this job. But I don't mind it. Taking out the trash is an excellent excuse to step outside and is one way Jenny and I team up—working smarter and not harder—to complete household chores.

Jenny, on the other hand, is in charge of weekly shopping and keeps our shared calendar up to date. These activities align with her organizational strengths. Although neither task is a highlight of Jenny's week, she would rather do them than pick up the pieces after I've given my best efforts.

Finally, some jobs energize. Jenny is a master in the kitchen, while I enjoy grilling. Because we both love to cook, we share this duty. Jenny does most of the cooking in the winter—when the Minnesota snow makes barbequing difficult. The tasty soups and hotdishes she whips up on frigid days are delicious.

I, on the other hand, step up during the warmer months—when operating the grill is invigorating. If you ever visit Minnesota in the summer, let me know, and I'll toss an extra burger, steak, or cheesy brat on the grill for you!

Because Jenny and I know ourselves and know each other, we divide up household chores in three powerful ways:

1. We take responsibility for tasks that play to our strengths.
2. We delegate frustrating tasks to the least offended person. The two of us see this as an excellent way to serve.
3. We share the fun household jobs that energize.

Although there is no perfect way to divide chores, when you know yourself and your spouse, these jobs are more enjoyable. To complete *The Couple's Chore Challenge,* use the prompts provided to examine which household tasks you like and dislike the most. Then dive into the *Chore Challenge Conversation Starters.* These chore-related questions will help the two of you know yourselves and lead yourselves well.

The Couple's Chore Challenge for Her

Three chores I don't mind doing are:

    1. _____
    2. _____
    3. _____

A chore that energizes me is:

    1. _____

The three household tasks I like least are:

    1. _____
    2. _____
    3. _____

Of my disliked chores, the most painful is:

    1. _____

The two of us might better divide household tasks in the future by _____
_____
_____

The Couple's Chore Challenge for Him

Three chores I don't mind doing are:

1. _____
2. _____
3. _____

A chore that energizes me is:

1. _____

The three household tasks I like least are:

1. _____
2. _____
3. _____

Of my disliked chores, the most painful is:

1. _____

The two of us might better divide household tasks in the future by _____
_____
_____

Chore Challenge Conversation Starters

Use the conversation starters below to tackle everyday tasks together. Take turns asking your spouse the following questions:

- Did anything surprise you about the chores I like and dislike? If so, what?

- Did you learn anything new about yourself during this challenge? If so, what was it?

- Based on our answers, do you think we should divide household tasks different than we do now? If so, what do you think the two of us could do better?

Day 13:
Celebrating the Unfair

"That's so unfair!" If you ever said these words, they probably carried a negative connotation. Typically, we use the word *unfair* to compare ourselves to people who have more than us or who have something better. But have you ever noticed that life is also unfair in our favor?

For example:

- It's unfair that I was born in the United States—one of the freest and wealthiest nations in the world.
- It's unfair that I get to be married to Jenny. My first marriage was a disaster, and life does not owe me a second chance. But in spite of my messy past, our relationship is amazing!
- It's also unfair that when I fail, Jenny still cheers me on.

By *unfair* I mean that I am not entitled to these blessings. Life is unfair to my advantage, and I am incredibly grateful for this.

When I was in junior high, our youth pastor told a story that stuck with me. It was about two prisoners who shared the same cell. Their meager living space only contained two cots and a tiny window. Each night, the first man would lay on his bunk and stare at the steel bars, which were a harsh reminder of his captivity. As he reflected on how unfair he perceived his life to be, he grew increasingly bitter.

But the second prisoner gazed beyond the bars, to a few stars that glimmered on the horizon. He reflected on past blessings and reminded himself that one day he would be free again. This prisoner drifted to sleep with renewed hope.

What each man fixated on made all the difference. In marriage, what you and I focus on also matters. Will we concentrate on circumstances that are unfair to our detriment, or will we center our attention on areas that are unfair in our favor?

Everyone has bars and stars in their life. Like the first prisoner, we can feed our bitterness by dwelling on past pain. Or, we can turn our attention to where life is unfair to our advantage and allow our joy to grow.

Instead of trying to right every wrong, let's celebrate the multitude of blessings we have. In *The Unfair Challenge,* concentrate on ways your relationship is unfair in your favor. I know that life has given me an abundance of good things I didn't earn and don't deserve. I believe the same is true for you.

The Unfair Challenge for Her

Complete this challenge by writing your spouse a love note. Describe some ways your relationship is unfair in your favor. Then, thank him for adding so much value to you.

_____

_____

_____

_____

_____

_____

_____

_____

_____

_____

_____

_____

_____

_____

_____

_____

_____

_____

The Unfair Challenge for Him

Complete this challenge by writing your spouse a love note. Describe some ways your relationship is unfair in your favor. Then, thank her for adding so much value to you.

_____

_____

_____

_____

_____

_____

_____

_____

_____

_____

_____

_____

_____

_____

_____

_____

_____

_____

_____

_____

Day 14:
Isolating Problems

I have good news for you. Your loved one is not the problem, and you are not the problem. The real problem is the problem itself. Now, let's look at some typical issues couples face.

Common relationship problems include:

- **Busyness:** As mentioned earlier, busyness is the new smoking. Rushing from one activity to the next is detrimental to relationships because it thwarts connection. Yet many people get caught up in the hustle and bustle anyway.

- **Stress:** If you and your loved one are stressed, then congratulations—you are normal. Although couples have more opportunities than ever before, an abundance of choices also increases stress, and a buildup of stress only hurts our bond.

- **Disagreements:** You have probably heard that opposites attract, and this is true. But opposite ideas also lead to quarrels. On the downside, research shows that most people don't change. Instead of accepting their partner as is—flaws and all—many couples become trapped in reoccurring disputes.

Obviously, this list could go on, but here is the bottom line: Neither you nor your loved one's name is anywhere on this list. Each difficulty is a problem, and not a person.

One of my favorite college professors said, "The only reason we make our loved one wrong is to make ourselves right." I think he is on to something. So, instead of attacking your spouse, isolate the problem by giving it a name. The specific issue can be any of the following:

- busyness
- stress
- different tastes
- lateness
- poor communication
- unfinished chores
- that fighting thing we do

The key is to direct our pent-up hurt away from our spouse and toward the problem. This makes it easier for our loved ones to lower their defenses and team up with us. Then, we can combat this foe together.

Here is a breakdown of the specific steps to take:

1. Isolate the problem by assigning it a name.
2. When discussing issues, avoid the words *you*, *your*, *his*, and *her*. For example, *your lateness* is not the problem. Instead, *lateness* is your arch nemesis.
3. Finally, take a cue from the Avengers, and team up to banish this foe.

In *The Isolate-the-Problem Challenge,* each of you will choose one problem to work on. Then ward off these adversaries together. Use the prompts on the next page to get started.

The Isolate-the-Problem Challenge for Her

Honey, I know that you are not the problem. Instead, the problem is the problem. A difficulty I would like to tackle together is our archnemesis of _____

_____

One way I will help fight off this foe is by____

_____

_____

One way you can help me battle this issue is by _____

_____

Combatting this enemy together means a lot to me because_____

_____

_____

_____

_____

_____

_____

The Isolate-the-Problem Challenge for Him

Honey, I know that you are not the problem. Instead, the problem is the problem. A difficulty I would like to tackle together is our archnemesis of _____

_____

One way I will help fight off this foe is by____

_____

_____

One way you can help me battle this issue is by _____

_____

Combatting this enemy together means a lot to me because_____

_____

_____

_____

_____

_____

_____

Day 15:
Don't Communicate,
Connecticate

I once had the privilege of speaking with family experts Gil and Brenda Stuart on a podcast. During our conversation, this husband and wife team introduced me to a powerful new word. Out of the blue, Gil dropped the term *connecticate*. This brilliant expression is formed from the words *connection* and *communication*.

I was enthralled! I felt like Luke Skywalker watching Yoda use the force or Daniel LaRusso seeing Mr. Miyagi perform the crane technique for the first time. I was in the presence of a wordsmithing master!

According to *Safe Haven Marriage*, "The greatest predictor of marital satisfaction and longevity is the presence of trust, emotional availability, and sensitive response."[4] The term *connecticate* captures all three concepts.

Connectication builds trust. It is founded on emotional availability and requires a sensitive response. This is a significant shift away from the old way of thinking which focused on improving communication alone.

A Better Way

In the past, experts believed if couples communicated clearly, then they would successfully navigate differences. Today, we know this doesn't work. Most longstanding disputes can't be solved.

Reoccurring arguments are rooted in fundamental differences, which makes change difficult. Some couples reach a workable solution for a time, but when the issue returns, so do the arguments. Other couples replace disagreements with icy coldness. The cycle goes like this:

1. Couples learn new skills that help them communicate better. Yelling is replaced with logic and compromise and eventually an agreement is reached.

2. Despite their agreement, one partner is frustrated but attempts to maintain the peace.

3. The internal friction causes the couple to disconnect. Their separation grows until an icy chill envelops the relationship.

I have seen this pattern play out in far too many marriages. These couples look sunny on the outside but feel gloomy on the inside. I have watched couples I respect post pictures of amazing family vacations on social media. By all outward appearances, everything seems to be going their way. Then they divorce a few months later. This is a good indication a hidden coldness was at work.

Clear communication helps couples to argue better, but it rarely leads to lasting success. This is why connectication is better than communication alone. When couples connecticate, genuinely happy moments occur.

The limited power of communication makes sense. When I ask couples how they fell in love, they never say, "We love each other because we communicate so well." Instead, couples share heartwarming stories of powerful connection moments.

Couples come together and stay together because their hearts intertwine. In happy relationships, communication and connection are best friends. Couples come together out of joy and stay together out of joy.

Joy does not diminish the value of commitment but is an important part of it. In marriage, couples commit to uniting *for better or for worse*, and even in the *for worse* moments we can still create pockets of joy. Connectication only takes a minute and can happen:

- over morning coffee
- by playing a board game
- during a dinner date
- on a walk

- at a bonfire
- while cooking a meal together

Connectication comes in many forms. As long as the two of you are enjoying each other's presence you are doing things right. In *The Connectication Challenge*, move beyond mere communication and connecticate!

The Connectication Challenge for Her

Complete this challenge by creating a connectication moment. This can be as simple as bonding over coffee, dessert, or a favorite game. If the two of you are drawing closer together, then you are doing things right. Then complete the journal entry below.

Our connectication moment happened when

_____

What I appreciated about this time was

_____

_____

_____

_____

_____

_____

_____

_____

_____

_____

_____

_____

The Connectication Challenge for Him

Complete this challenge by creating a connectication moment. This can be as simple as bonding over coffee, dessert, or a favorite game. If the two of you are drawing closer together, then you are doing things right. Then complete the journal entry below.

Our connectication moment happened when

_____

What I appreciated about this time was

_____

_____

_____

_____

_____

_____

_____

_____

_____

_____

_____

_____

Day 16:
MTO Goals for Couples

"I've tried that, and it doesn't work." In my therapeutic work, I have heard this often. While some strategies don't resonate well, more often, relationships decay because the dosage is off. Just as a single spoonful of penicillin won't cure an infection, a lone act of kindness can't restore a broken bond. Relationship wounds are often greater than we realize.

Family therapist Virginia Satir said, "We need four hugs a day for survival. We need eight hugs a day for maintenance. We need twelve hugs a day for growth." Now that is some serious hugging. Virginia clearly understands the need to bond with our loved ones.

Based on this quote, I would guess Virginia's primary love language is physical touch. Her statement will resonate best with those who appreciate physical expressions of love. According to author Gary Chapman[5], the other love languages include:

- quality time
- receiving gifts
- words of affirmation
- acts of service

Although most people appreciate all five love languages, one characteristically stands out. For example, Jenny's primary love language is receiving gifts. Thoughtful presents cause her to light up in ways the other languages don't, and she remembers these tokens of affection long after I've forgotten them. I value physical touch, so I'm overjoyed each time Jenny takes my hand in hers.

Because each loving act draws couples closer, I believe Virginia's statement could be updated as follows: "We need four loving acts a day for survival. We need eight loving acts a day for maintenance. We need twelve loving acts a day for growth." So, don't be afraid to experiment with all five love languages. The key is to connect regularly and to speak your partner's primary language as often as possible.

MTO Goals for Couples

Virginia's statement is an excellent example of MTO goals. The letters *MTO* stand for *minimal*, *target*, and *optimal*. MTO goals are powerful because they allow for messy days.

Couples with MTO goals will commit to a minimum of four loving acts a day. This is the necessary dosage for survival and should serve as a last resort. Couples might use this minimum dose when

- both partners work overtime or are exceptionally busy
- one or both spouses are exhausted or sick
- everything that can go wrong does go wrong

On average days, you and your loved one will commit to eight loving acts — the amount needed for maintenance. Couples who bond this regularly make kindness the norm. On optimal days, you and your loved one will connect twelve times or more. According to Satir, this leads to growth and is the ultimate aim.

MTO Goals in Action

Recently, Jenny and I celebrated our seventh anniversary. We ate together, watched movies, talked, laughed, played games, held hands, and enjoyed one another's presence. I'm not sure how many moments of connection we had, but it far exceeded twelve.

I share this story because, for some couples, connecting twelve times a day may sound complicated. Yet, once this habit forms, the pattern is natural. Remember, each kind word, act of service, engaging text, gentle touch, and gift counts.

In *The MTO Connection Challenge*, put MTO goals to work. Experiment with all five love languages. Take note of the acts that bring your spouse the most joy. This will lead you to his or her primary language.

The MTO Connection Challenge for Her

How many connecting moments can you create? Check the boxes you complete. Bonus points for doing twelve or more!

- ☐ Hold his hand
- ☐ Listen attentively
- ☐ Write a love note
- ☐ Send an encouraging email
- ☐ Ask questions about his day
- ☐ Do a chore for him
- ☐ Give a hug
- ☐ Send a kind text
- ☐ Praise a job well done
- ☐ Give a massage
- ☐ Share a funny story
- ☐ Say, "I love you"
- ☐ Praise him in front of his friends
- ☐ Watch his favorite show with him
- ☐ Plan a surprise date
- ☐ Call just to let him know you care
- ☐ Ask him to choose today's activity
- ☐ Cook a favorite meal or dessert
- ☐ Be there when he needs you
- ☐ Give a thoughtful gift

The MTO Connection Challenge for Him

How many connecting moments can you create? Check the boxes you complete. Bonus points for doing twelve or more!

- ☐ Hold her hand
- ☐ Listen attentively
- ☐ Write a love note
- ☐ Send an encouraging email
- ☐ Ask questions about her day
- ☐ Do a chore for her
- ☐ Give a hug
- ☐ Send a kind text
- ☐ Praise a job well done
- ☐ Give a massage
- ☐ Share a funny story
- ☐ Say, "I love you"
- ☐ Praise her in front of her friends
- ☐ Watch her favorite show with her
- ☐ Plan a surprise date
- ☐ Call just to let her know you care
- ☐ Ask her to choose today's activity
- ☐ Cook a favorite meal or dessert
- ☐ Be there when she needs you
- ☐ Give a thoughtful gift

Day 17:
The Gift of Self-Care

Contrary to popular belief, self-care is not selfish. Instead, it's one of the best gifts we can give our loved one. In college, I made an impromptu stop at a fast-food restaurant. I was in a rush and noticed that the line for the drive-through wrapped around the building, but few people were inside.

To save time, I parked quickly, scrambled in, and placed my order. That's when I spotted a family friend huddled in a booth. I walked over and said hello in an attempt to be polite. This man, who I now saw was in a modified fetal position, replied, "Oh, hi. I'm just taking a minute to relax... you know... uh, to de-stress before heading home."

Everything about him screamed defeat. His gaze was distant. His voice was hollow and apologetic. Unsure of what to do next, I tried making small talk. Fortunately, for both of us, my order was ready fast. The two of us said awkward good-byes, and I darted out of the restaurant.

As I beelined to my car, I remembered overhearing a conversation my parents had a few weeks earlier. They mentioned this family was having marriage problems and difficulties with their kids—a double whammy of stress, I'm sure! This man was visibly drained, and my heart went out to him. This moment impacted me enough that I can easily recall it two decades later.

Contrast this with someone having a great day. This man walks through the door energized, kisses his spouse, and engages in conversation. How you and I show up makes an enormous difference. I love it when Jenny is refreshed. This is why I believe self-care is one of the best gifts we can give our spouse.

According to the diathesis-stress model of mental illness, if you and I don't manage stress well, we literally drive ourselves crazy. Each of us has a genetic propensity for mental illness. We also have a preset amount of stress we can bear. If tensions elevate above this level, then symptoms of mental illness set in.

So how good are you relaxing? Healthy self-care can be as simple as:

- Running, walking, or hiking. Nearly all physical exertion is excellent self-care.
- Reading a favorite book or watching a movie.
- Chatting with friends.
- Slowing down and breathing deeply.
- Laughing, even if this means finding the humor amid the chaos.

Perhaps you are already energized. Fantastic! Then your job is to keep this momentum going. On the other hand, if you feel like my family friend — utterly defeated — your job is to take care of yourself.

Emotions are contagious. Self-care allows us to be fully present and a catalyst for joy. Regardless of how you presently feel, there is hope. In *The Self-care Challenge*, assess your current level of stress. Then practice healthy self-care and get energized!

The Self-care Challenge for Her

For today's challenge, complete the self-care activities below.

Rate how you feel on a scale of one to ten. A one means *stressed*, and ten means *energized*. Right now, my overall energy is at a _____

List one to three things you will do to practice healthy self-care.

I will practice healthy self-care by _____

_____

Finally, complete the journal entry below.

Taking time for self-care will enrich my bond with my spouse because _____

_____

_____

_____

_____

_____

_____

_____

The Self-care Challenge for Him

For today's challenge, complete the self-care activities below.

Rate how you feel on a scale of one to ten. A one means *stressed,* and ten means *energized.* Right now, my overall energy is at a _____

List one to three things you will do today to practice healthy self-care.

I will practice healthy self-care by _____
_____

Finally, complete the journal entry below.

Taking time for self-care will enrich my bond with my spouse because _____
_____
_____
_____
_____
_____
_____

Day 18:
Rooted in Love

For nearly a decade, I served in children's ministry. My favorite object lesson involved hiding an object in my hand, describing it, and letting the kids guess what I held. Here are the clues I offered:

- This item is so small it fits in my closed hand.
- It's powerful enough to split an enormous rock in two.
- It is also perfectly safe.
- It's so safe you might sit on it or eat off of it.
- If you were a bird or a squirrel, you could even make this your home.

Do you know what the object is?

If you guessed a redwood seed, you are right. You may wonder how a redwood seed can do all these things. Here are the answers:

- A redwood seed is roughly half the size of an acorn, so it's easily concealed in a closed fist.
- Sometimes a lone seed falls into cracked rock. As the seed grows, the sapling splits the boulder in two.
- A fully-grown redwood can be fashioned into beautiful furniture — including tables and chairs.
- A mature tree makes an excellent home for birds and squirrels.

Of course, none of this happens fast, and the right environment is needed for the seed to grow. This includes good soil, plenty of sunlight, and fresh water.

Healthy relationships develop like a redwood. To flourish, an environment of trust, emotional availability, and sensitive responsiveness are required. These three ingredients are the primary factors in marital satisfaction. Each one is so vital it is worth examining alone.

Trust: Trust is the key to intimacy or into-me-see. Allowing our spouse to peer into our inner world takes vulnerability. If we are going to know our loved ones and be known, then trust is a must.

Emotional Availability: This means we are ready and able to connect. In times of distress, our spouse doesn't have to wonder, *Will my loved one hold me tight?* We are a safe haven amid life's storms.

Sensitive Responsiveness: A sensitive, responsive spouse is open to verbal and nonverbal cues. Is your loved one looking for a listening ear, encouragement, comfort, or advice? The sensitive spouse knows — or is wise enough to ask.

Nature has its dry seasons, which is why the healthiest redwoods develop deep roots. Dry spells happen for couples too. Trust gets broken. Couples become snippy and respond harshly.

A key to withstanding dry seasons is to get deeply rooted in love. Do this by making trust, emotional availability, and sensitive responsiveness the norm. In *The Rooted-in-Love Challenge*, identify which key area is your strength and which has the most opportunity for growth. Then take one small step toward becoming more deeply rooted than ever before.

The Rooted-in-Love Challenge for Her

Use the prompts provided to complete today's challenge.

Place a check next to your current strength:

☐ Trust
☐ Emotional availability
☐ Sensitive responsiveness

Check the box where you would like to grow:

☐ Trust
☐ Emotional availability
☐ Sensitive responsiveness

Decide how you will grow in one of these areas and complete the statement below. For example, "I will nurture our relationship in the area of *trust* by *listening attentively to my loved one as he talks about his day.*"

I will nurture our relationship in the area of _____ by _____

_____

The Rooted-in-Love Challenge for Him

Use the prompts provided to complete today's challenge.

Place a check next to your current strength:

- ☐ trust
- ☐ emotional availability
- ☐ sensitive responsiveness

Check the box where you would like to grow:

- ☐ trust
- ☐ emotional availability
- ☐ sensitive responsiveness

Decide how you will grow in one of these areas and complete the statement below. For example, "I will nurture our relationship in the area of *trust* by *listening attentively to my loved one as he talks about his day.*"

I will nurture our relationship in the area of _____ by _____
_____

Day 19:
Capture Your
Spouse's Heart

If your loved one wanted to capture your heart, what should he or she put underneath this box trap?

Although this question may sound odd, it's a good one—I promise! I am trying to improve at buying Jenny gifts. Not expensive gifts, but simple ones like:

- flowers
- cards
- chocolates
- items I know she needs

- anything that lets Jenny know I'm thinking of her

Although I'm not good at this yet, I am getting better. At the beginning of the year, Jenny let me know her primary love language is gifts. In other words, when Jenny receives a present, she feels especially loved.

I'm glad she told me. As a guy, I like it when Jenny helps me connect the dots. Plus, being able to talk about our needs is a sign of a healthy relationship.

For today's challenge, make connecting easy for your loved one by sharing the small things you enjoy most. The best way for a couple to stay happily married is for each partner to keep doing the things that brought them together in the first place. Of course, this makes a lot of sense.

When I asked Jenny, "What drew you to me before we got married?" she reminded me of the unique cards I sent and the thoughtful gifts I gave. Jenny has kept many of these tokens of my affection to this day.

When I ask other couples what gifts they appreciate most, I receive a variety of answers. This demonstrates the value of *The Platinum Rule,* which states we ought to love others in the ways they want to be loved.

How do you want your partner to demonstrate love? What should he or she put underneath a box trap to guarantee your capture? In *The Heart-trap Challenge*, there is a separate space for each of you. Write down four ways your loved one can capture your heart. Give yourself bonus points if you fill in all eight blanks.

The Heart-trap Challenge for Her

What should your loved one put in a box trap
if he wants to guarantee your capture?

1. _____
2. _____
3. _____
4. _____
5. _____
6. _____
7. _____
8. _____

The Heart-trap Challenge for Him

What should your loved one put in a box trap
if she wants to guarantee your capture?

1. _____
2. _____
3. _____
4. _____
5. _____
6. _____
7. _____
8. _____

Day 20:
Inspiring Change

Blaise Pascal said, "When we are in love, we seem to ourselves quite different from what we were before." And he is right! Because of Jenny, I have grown in the following ways:

- I am able to relax my tight budgeting for amazing family adventures.
- I am better at organizing and planning.
- My parenting has improved in hundreds of big and small ways.

Uniting our lives allowed me to flourish. I not only seem quite different, I am quite different. It's not that Jenny set out to change me. It's simply that being around her influenced change. Family therapists refer to this as the ripple effect. When a tiny pebble is tossed into a pond, it produces ripples that extend to the shore. Similarly, it is impossible to live with someone—day in and day out—and not change.

If you want your spouse to improve, I am all for it. Just know there are right ways and wrong ways to go about this. The right way is to be the pebble that starts the ripple. Here are three steps to take.

1. **Begin with you.** Families are systems. Much like a bowl of spaghetti, family members' lives intertwine. It's impossible for one person to change without others having to adjust. This means the best way to influence your spouse is to begin with you.

2. **Encourage and praise.** Animals learn faster when rewarded for positive behaviors than when punished for negative ones. This strategy works with humans too. Punishing only escalates conflict, while catching our loved one doing things right and sending heaps of praise their way influences change.

3. **Shape.** According to psychology, shaping is another powerful behavior-altering tool. Shaping happens when we rejoice over small milestones. For example, if your family wants to reduce spending, try celebrating the time your spouse places a pack of gum back on the shelf while in the checkout line. Even if it's not the massive savings you hoped for, it is a step in the right direction.

Wrong Ways to Inspire Change

William Glasser, the founder of Choice Theory, has a unique term for trying to force change. He calls this *external control psychology*. Examples of external control psychology include:

- blaming and shaming one's spouse
- yelling and fighting
- punishing our loved one — including withdrawing emotionally

- acting like our partner is fully responsible for problems while ignoring positive steps we can take

We always options, but external control psychology ignores them and places the full responsibility on our spouse. If external control psychology does produce a desired result, our relationship is scarred in the process — so no one wins. In *The Inspire Change Challenge*, focus on what you can do, and be the pebble that sends ripples of positive influence into your relationship.

The Inspire Change Challenge for Her

Use the prompts below to complete today's challenge.

Describe three ways your loved one inspired you to change for the better:

1. _____
   _____
2. _____
   _____
3. _____
   _____

List three things you are doing (or plan to do) to inspire joyful change in your home:

1. _____
   _____
2. _____
   _____
3. _____
   _____

The Inspire Change Challenge for Him

Use the prompts below to complete today's challenge.

Describe three ways your loved one inspired you to change for the better:

1. _____
   _____

2. _____
   _____

3. _____
   _____

List three things you are doing (or plan to do) to inspire joyful change in your home:

1. _____
   _____

2. _____
   _____

3. _____
   _____

Day 21:
Getting Honest
with Heart Talk

"How's your heart?" A couple I know uses this question to draw each other out. It's an excellent way to get a quick temperature reading on your relationship, and I suggest asking it often. But what about times when something is amiss, and our partner doesn't ask?

It's been said that holding on to bitterness is as absurd as drinking poison and hoping the other person gets sick. Allowing frustrations to fester is obviously not the answer. But if we confront issues head on, we run the risk of stirring up trouble.

This chapter contains a simple blueprint for sharing one's heart. The formula has four parts and goes like this:

When you _____, I feel _____ because _____. In the future, I would like _____.

Let's examine each key area.

"When you _____"

This phrase isolates the problem with statements like:

- come home late
- don't tell me the schedule in advance
- ignore me in front of your friends
- overspend
- play on your phone while I'm talking to you

The purpose is to pinpoint the exact issue. Isolating the problem is essential because your spouse is not the problem, and you are not the problem. Instead, the problem is the problem. Once it is clearly defined, the two of you can attack the difficulty together.

"I feel _____"

The goal of this phrase is to create awareness of how the problem impacts you. Good feeling words include:

- scared
- worried
- sad
- hurt

Although there are other options, I suggest staying away from *anger*. A deeper emotion is always present. In heart-talks, we want to get to the root cause. Plus, anger is directed at our spouse, while other emotions focus on the problem. Taking a break from anger helps our loved ones to lower their defenses and team up with us.

"because _____"

This is your opportunity to dive into into-me-see. Build your loved one up by expressing just how much he or she means to you. Nearly all problems are relationship problems. This issue probably causes you to feel disconnected from your spouse. Explain how this separation hurts. You might say something like, "When you came home late..."

- I felt lonely because I was looking forward to spending the evening with you.
- I felt worried because I thought you might be hurt.
- I felt sad because I cooked your favorite meal, and I was looking forward to enjoying it together.

"In the future, I would like _____"

Now turn your attention toward solutions. If we aim at nothing, we'll hit it every time. By entering the conversation with a solution ready, we offer hope. Just remember, this statement isn't a demand. It's only one possible resolution. If your partner isn't agreeable, the next step is to brainstorm more ideas.

This formula has the power to bring clarity fast, but it also has two drawbacks. First, when spoken verbatim, it can sound robotic. Second, lots of meaning is packed into this short phrase. Receiving this much information at once can feel overwhelming.

I suggest using this formula to gain clarity before your heart-talk. Think of it as heart-talk training wheels. Let the key points guide your conversation while using your own words.

A final key is to slow the conversation down. You've thought about the problem for a while, while your partner may still be coming to terms with its severity. So be sure to give your spouse plenty of time to process what you say. Although this phrase doesn't guarantee success, it is an excellent way to share your heart while focusing on the problem.

There are two ways you can complete *The Heart-talk Challenge*. The first option is to ask your loved one, "How's your heart?" Then, listen empathetically. Option two is to apply the heart-talk formula to a current issue. Know these talks can feel awkward at first but get easier with practice. After your heart-talk, use the conversation starters on the next page to refine your heart-talk skills.

The Heart-talk Challenge
for Him and Her

Complete this challenge by using the conversation starters below to refine your heart-talk:

- What do you think went well in our heart-talk?

- What do you think you could have done better?

- What do you think I could have done better?

- Did you feel this conversation moved too fast, too slow, or at just the right pace?

- How did using the heart-talk formula bring clarity?

- Do you have ideas on how we can have better heart-talks in the future?

Day 22:
Why Couples Argue

"Why do couples argue?" our group leader asked. "I'll show you. But first, I need an assistant." I was on the edge of my seat, eager to see how this demonstration played out.

A volunteer strolled to the front of the room, and the leader asked her to hold up her hands. Without warning, he placed his palms against hers and began to push. A look of confusion crossed the woman's face as she found herself being backed into a corner—literally!

Realizing what was happening, the woman planted her feet and pushed back. "OK, OK," the leader said. "Let's pause the experiment." He asked the class to describe what they saw, and an insightful discussion followed. Yet, one key element was missed. "Did anyone notice our volunteer smile? For a brief moment, she was having fun. Her smile was quick, but I assure you, it was there." The leader then suggested a repeat of the experiment.

He asked the woman to hold up her hands again. This time she also extended her back foot. A fierce determination flashed in her eyes which communicated, "You better get ready because this time I'm going to back you into a corner." The leader started counting down. "Three... two... one... Oh, never mind. Let's not do a repeat."

The class watched in awe as an unmistakable look of disappointment crossed this woman's face. Point proved! This time, the volunteer was clearly looking forward to the thrill of the fight.

Arguments can be exhilarating for married couples too. Quarrels get our adrenaline flowing and give us something to talk about. When couples argue, they engage, connect, and hone their wit. Please don't misunderstand. I'm not suggesting couples like everything about arguing. I am merely pointing out that secondary gains exist.

In prison, solitary confinement is the harshest form of punishment. In marriage, a disgruntled connection is better than no connection at all. One reason unhappy couples fight is to get their connection and excitement needs met. Happy couples meet these same needs in kind, healthy ways.

Although couples argue for many reasons, I've listed four common ones below. Unhappy couples fight because:

- Fighting is one way they get their excitement and connection need met.
- Arguing makes them feel right. A favorite college professor used to say, "Couples try to make their spouse wrong to make themselves right."
- Fighting is a habit, and habits are hard to break.
- One person feels powerless and tries to convince the other person to take responsibility.

This isn't to suggest all arguing is wrong. Strong emotions are like a car's warning light—they indicate something needs to be addressed. Ignoring problems and blowing up over them are two unhealthy extremes.

The good news is that couples caught in conflict can break the cycle by forming new habits. Use the prompts on the next page to complete *The Fighting-fair Challenge*. First, see if any of the unnecessary reasons couples fight apply to you. Then increase your joy by finding happier alternatives.

The Fighting-fair Challenge for Her

1. In our relationship, we occasionally argue to get connection or excitement needs met.

Yes / No

If yes, how else can you meet this need?

_____

2. In our relationship, we sometimes argue because I want to be right.

Yes / No

If yes, what new strategy will you use to feel right? _____

3. In our relationship, we sometimes argue because it's a habit.

Yes / No

If yes, what new habit will you replace this with? _____

4. In our relationship, we sometimes argue because I feel powerless.

Yes / No

If yes, what other actions can you take to feel more   powerful?   _____

_____

The Fighting-fair Challenge for Him

1. In our relationship, we occasionally argue to get connection or excitement needs met.

Yes / No

If yes, how else can you meet this need?

_____

2. In our relationship, we sometimes argue because I want to be right.

Yes / No

If yes, what new strategy will you use to feel right? _____

3. In our relationship, we sometimes argue because it's a habit.

Yes / No

If yes, what new habit will you replace this with? _____

4. In our relationship, we sometimes argue because I feel powerless.

Yes / No

If yes, what other actions can you take to feel more   powerful?   _____

_____

Day 23:
Creating Peak Moments

I pull Addison snugly to my side as our circular raft enters the winding tube slide. Addison's older sisters shriek with delight at the first drop. *This is going to be fun!* I think to myself.

We pick up speed — a lot of speed! I clutch Addison tighter, doing my best to keep us both inside with my free hand. As we round the next bend, our raft shoots halfway up the side, stopping just short of flipping over. We drop abruptly, followed by more screams, and slide even faster. After navigating several more turns, the four of us burst through the waterfall at the end of the ride.

That was a lot rougher than I expected. I hope little Addison is OK, I think to myself. Addison sputters, pushing her sopping hair out of her face, and whispers, "Daddy, let's do it again!" After a second trip down the massive slide, we reunite with Jenny, who is enjoying the quality, one-on-one time with our youngest daughter. The six of us gingerly float down the lazy river and duck under waves in the wave pool before returning to our room. That evening, we meet up with other hotel guests for a family dance party. Then our older girls participate in a massive scavenger hunt. Jenny and I smile. We love watching our children have fun and know this adventure will be long remembered.

In *The Power of Moments,* Chip and Dan Heath write, "Defining moments shape our lives, but we don't have to wait for them to happen. We can be the authors of them." If you have kids, you'll want to create two distinct types of peak moments—peak moments with your family and peak moments with your spouse.[6]

In addition to annual family trips, Jenny and I plan at least one getaway for just the two of us. We believe physical gifts are nice, but adventures are better. These trips are always a highlight of the year.

Two years ago, Jenny and I explored the Minnesota skyways—one of the longest elevated walkways in the world. This year, we relaxed at a favorite resort. These getaways are easy to plan because they involve plenty of sleeping and free time. With six active children at home, creating space for uninterrupted time together is what matters most.

Couples need to celebrate their relationships and should never stop looking for ways to keep their bond exhilarating. Before marriage, adventures like paragliding, paddle boarding, long walks on the beach, and exploring the town were an integral part of our dating experience. But the adventures shouldn't end with the words *I do*.

The peak experiences you and your spouse create will vary depending on your tastes and season of life. What's most important is to keep the peak moments going and to never allow the adventures to end.

In *The Peak Moment Challenge,* reflect on past peak experiences. Then brainstorm future peak moments and decide how you will make these dreams a reality!

The Peak Moments Challenge
for Her and Him

Use the prompts below to complete today's challenge.

List three peak moments you and your spouse had in the past.

1._____
2._____
3_____

Write down three peak experiences you would like to have in the future.

1._____
2._____
3_____

What small steps will you take to bring one of these peak moments into fruition?

1._____
2._____
3_____

Day 24: Connecting Like Velcro

There are many things I appreciate about Jenny. One of my favorites is that when I reach for her, Jenny reaches back. I've heard this type of bond described as a Velcro relationship.

If you examine two strips of Velcro, you'll notice one strip contains hundreds of tiny hooks while the other is made up of many small loops. This intricate system is what allows Velcro to connect, disconnect, and reconnect with ease.

These hooks and loops stretch out over time—to the point they appear to be reaching for one another. Like Velcro, happy couples also connect, disconnect, and reach out.

Let's begin with disconnection. Couples separate in three primary ways. First, they detach physically. Perhaps one partner leaves on work trip or needs to care for an aging parent. Physical distance is usually the least damaging. When a strong emotional bond is present, couples feel close even when they are miles apart.

A second type of detachment is emotional separation. This can be caused by arguments and lingering resentment. Finally, a buildup of stress may cause a couple to mentally disconnect. Men, for example, are infamous for checking out inside of their "man caves."

Although moments of disconnection are normal, staying apart for long hurts. Physical pain and emotional distress cause the same areas of our brain to activate. In other words, relationships are like food, water, shelter, and oxygen. The human brain sees these bonds as a survival need.

If all couples connected, disconnected, and reconnected as easily as Velcro, there would be far fewer divorces. The bad news is that you and I cannot make our loved one connect.

We can, however, courageously reach out. Reaching is as simple as

- a hug
- a kind word
- a gentle touch
- a soft smile
- engaging conversation
- an inside joke

Reaching for your loved one is a win, regardless of how he or she responds, and usually the more mature partner reaches out first.

What I love about my relationship with Jenny is that reaching has become a part of our routine. We intentionally built connection moments into our day and they are now a habit. Each morning, Jenny and I connect over coffee. We reconnect again after work, and when the children fall asleep, the final moments of the day are reserved only for us.

Some days these times are long. The two of us watch a movie, play a game, have dessert, or relax by the fire. During life's busy seasons, these connection moments are reduced to a quick hug and a hello. Either way, the pattern of dropping everything—even if only for a moment—is constant.

One of the best ways to form a new habit is to attach the desired practice to a routine that already exists. This is how I published twenty books in just over six years. I connected my writing time to my daily coffee-brewing routine.

Every morning, my alarm sounds at 4:30 a.m. After rolling out of bed, I brew a pot of coffee, start a fire, turn on music, and write. Even if I only squeak out a few lines, those words add up.

The benefits of connecting with our loved one compounds over time. Jenny and I are now in the habit of reconnecting after each separation, and any break in this routine feels weird. In happy relationships a kind connection is normal. So make connecting a habit.

In *The Velcro Challenge*, rate how well you and your spouse connect. Then brainstorm ways to start your own connection routine.

The Velcro Challenge for Her

On a scale of one to ten, how good are you at reaching for your spouse? A one means "I seldom reach out," while a ten means "I reach out often." Write your number here _____

On a scale of one to ten, how good are you at reaching back when your loved one reaches for you? A one means "I rarely reach back," while a ten indicates "I respond by reaching back quickly." Write your number here _____

Finally, have you and your loved one developed a connection habit? If not, think of three times you plan to reach out in the future. Then follow the habit-building method of attaching your new habit to one that is already formed. Use the prompts below to get started.

1. I will reach for my partner after _____
2. I will reach for my partner after _____
3. I will reach for my partner after _____

The Velcro Challenge for Him

On a scale of one to ten, how good are you at reaching for your spouse? A one means "I seldom reach out," while a ten means "I reach out often." Write your number here _____

On a scale of one to ten, how good are you at reaching back when your loved one reaches for you? A one means "I rarely reach back," while a ten indicates "I respond by reaching back quickly." Write your number here _____

Finally, have you and your loved one developed a connection habit? If not, think of three times you plan to reach out in the future. Then follow the habit-building method of attaching your new habit to one that is already formed. Use the prompts below to get started.

1. I will reach for my partner after _____
2. I will reach for my partner after _____
3. I will reach for my partner after _____

Day 25:
Extreme Ownership
in Marriage

With so many people eager to blame others, the concept of extreme ownership is huge. In *Extreme Ownership: How U.S. Navy SEALs Lead and Win*, authors Jocko Willink and Leif Babin write, "Leaders must own everything in their world. There is no one else to blame."[7]

The authors aren't suggesting we cause every negative situation to happen. Many events are outside of our control. Instead, extreme ownership means taking full responsibility for our response. Other people bemoan their unfortunate circumstances, but extreme owners take responsibility and act. Extreme ownership has many applications and is a powerful principle for Navy SEALs, business professionals, and for couples.

I once heard a pastor share how extreme ownership saved his marriage. Their wedding was a dream come true. However, shortly after the ceremony, the dresser drawers nearly caused their relationship to crumble.

The conflict began the morning this new husband groggily made his way to the bathroom. Suddenly, "Bam!" he slammed his shin on an open dresser drawer. After howling in pain, the pastor chided his wife for leaving the drawer open. She vowed never to repeat the offense. In spite of her sincerity, it wasn't long before this old habit returned.

The pastor complained, scolded, and chided. His wife vowed to change, but it was never long before the problem resurfaced. The dresser drawers soon became a significant source of tension in their marriage.

After months of arguing, the couple reached the end of their rope. The pastor decided he banged his shin for the last time.

After howling in pain, he felt a bubbling rage and slammed the dresser shut!

That's when he had an epinine. This pastor realized he deeply loved his wife. He also saw that by closing the drawer himself, he solved his own problem. *From now on, I am going to take 100 percent responsibility for shutting the drawers,* he thought. *And every time I close a drawer, I'm going to remind myself how much I love my wife.*

This is extreme ownership at its best! The pastor saw he had two options. He could keep trying to change his wife—which wasn't working. Or, out of genuine love, he could take ownership for the problem. He chose the latter, and the dresser drawers were never an issue again.

The principle of extreme ownership has many names:

- In business, it's called "controlling the controllables."

- A coach for the Minnesota Vikings teaches the team to "dominate the controllables," which makes perfect sense in football.
- My friend Erik, who mentors teenagers, prefers the phrase, "You always have a choice."

Certain aspects of every situation are under our control. Exasperated couples can choose one or more of the following solutions:

- You can talk to your loved one about the problem.
- You can solve the issue yourself.
- You can hire someone to do a job you both dislike.
- You can enlist the help of a pastor, counselor, coach, or another trained professional.
- You can read relationship books to discover how other couples solved a similar issue.
- You can take a break from the difficulty to reconnect.

These are just a few of the controllables. Of course, you can also endlessly argue about the problem, and this too is a choice. The point is, you and I always have a choice. Just understand that trying to change your spouse is not extreme ownership. Placing blame is an attempt to get someone else to own the issue, and this is a recipe for conflict.

To complete *The Extreme Ownership Challenge*, identify a current problem. List four steps you can take to move toward resolution and take extreme ownership!

The Extreme Ownership Challenge for Her

Describe a current relationship difficulty:

_____

_____

Brainstorm five actions you can take to resolve this issue.

1. _____
2. _____
3. _____
4. _____
5. _____

Choose one idea you will apply immediately and complete the extreme ownership declaration below.

I will take extreme ownership for_____

_____ by

_____

Now, put your plan into action and take extreme ownership!

The Extreme Ownership Challenge for Him

Describe a current relationship difficulty:

_____

_____

Brainstorm five actions you can take to resolve this issue.

1. _____
2. _____
3. _____
4. _____
5. _____

Choose one idea you will apply immediately and complete the extreme ownership declaration below.

I will take extreme ownership for_____

_____ by

_____

Now, put your plan into action and take extreme ownership!

Day 26:
Influencing Positive Change

It only takes one person to change a relationship. If you toss a pebble into a pond it sends ripples all the way to shore. Similarly, when one person makes a positive change, his or her partner must adjust. It's impossible for two people to live under the same roof and not influence each other.

Thanks to neuroscience, we have new insights into how this ripple effect works. In 1992, researchers accidentally discovered the presence of mirror neurons. The discovery happened when a neuroscientist mapped a monkey's brain while eating an ice-cream cone. He noticed the monkey's brain lit up as if he was enjoying the treat. This led to the discovery of mirror neurons in monkeys, and similar neurons were later found in humans.

Mirror neurons fire both when an action is performed and observed. The impact of mirror neurons is everywhere. Shortly after my daughter, Emmalynn, was born, I tried a simple mirror neuron experiment. I looked Emma in the eyes and stuck out my tongue. Thanks to mirror neurons, Emma stuck her tongue out right back. Another simple experiment is to smile at a stranger. If you catch someone's eye, chances are they will return your smile.

Mirror neurons are the foundation of empathy. Perhaps you heard that attitudes are more often caught than taught. Now we know why. Thanks to mirror neurons, one person is all it takes to raise the emotional temperature in a relationship.

When my girls were younger, they would squeal with delight, "Daddy's home!" the moment I walked through the door. No matter how tired I was, their enthusiastic outburst always renewed my joy.

For anyone who feels alone in bettering their relationship, mirror neurons offer hope. One person is all it takes to increase marital joy. This can be done through:

- kind words
- a warm embrace
- greeting your partner with a smile first thing in the morning and last thing at night
- asking thought-provoking questions that communicate "I care about you"
- turning your full attention toward your spouse
- reaching out to end an argument, even if your loved one doesn't reach back

Ice melts at exactly 32 degrees. At 31 degrees, water remains solid. Ice has a specific tipping point, and so does joy. Melting a loved one's frozen heart will require more than a smile or two. Becoming joyfully married requires ongoing effort. But keep going because that tipping point is within reach.

According to Ross Perot, "Most people give up just when they're about to achieve success. They quit on the one-yard line. They give up at the last minute of the game one foot from a winning touchdown." I believe he's right.

While there is nothing wrong with hoping that one day your partner is as passionate about growth as you are, why not start with you? Instead of hoping things get better, be the pebble that sends ripples of positive change into your relationship. Attitudes are contagious, and one person can be a catalyst for joy.

If you and your loved one are reading this book together, then you already have an advantage. You are both interested in bettering your relationship. Still, it's common for one partner to feel more passionate about growth than the other. If you want your spouse to change, great, I'm all for it. Just know the best place to begin is with you. In *The Pebble Challenge*, focus on the positive actions you can take, and raise the emotional temperature of your bond.

The Pebble Challenge for Her

Be the pebble that sends ripples of joy into your relationship. List ten things you can do to increase the happiness in your marriage. Bonus points for filling in all twelve blanks!

1. _____

2. _____

3. _____

4. _____

5. _____

6. _____

7. _____

8. _____

9. _____

10. _____

11. _____

12. _____

The Pebble Challenge for Him

Be the pebble that sends ripples of joy into your relationship. List ten things you can do to increase the happiness in your marriage. Bonus points for filling in all twelve blanks!

1. _____
2. _____
3. _____
4. _____
5. _____
6. _____
7. _____
8. _____
9. _____
10. _____
11. _____
12. _____

Day 27:
Creating a Heroic Union

Marriage is not a four-letter word, but you wouldn't know this from the looks on many people's faces. Words like *marriage conference*, *relationship book*, and *couple's seminar* trigger a blank, deer-in-the-headlights gaze.

The sad truth is there is a severe shortage of heroic marriages. I define a heroic marriage as a relationship so amazing that other couples exclaim, "That is what I want!" So where are the Michael Jordan's of relationships — the marriages so amazing they inspire others?

One of my favorite Michael Jordan quotes is "I've missed more than nine thousand shots in my career. I've lost almost three hundred games. Twenty-six times I've been trusted to take the game-winning shot and missed. I've failed over and over and over again in my life. And that is why I succeed."

Michael Jordan's honesty is refreshing, and heroic couples don't wear a mask of perfection either. Real life is messy. Couples are going to argue, rub each other the wrong way, and fail.

Rough patches don't mean the two of you are incompatible. Rather, they are quite normal. In heroic marriages, couples mess up, get back up, and reconnect again. In the best unions, partners find reasons to celebrate amid the storms.

Some studies suggest the rate of divorce is subsiding. But experts don't view this as positive. After the current generation witnessed countless failed marriages and couples white-knuckling-it through their relationship, they have become disillusioned with wedlock. The younger generation is choosing cohabitation over marriage, and fewer weddings means less divorce.

Redefining a Joyful Marriage

Elizabeth Gilbert said, "To be fully seen by somebody, then, and be loved anyhow — this is a human offering that can border on miraculous." In a miraculous marriage, each person is fully known and completely accepted — flaws and all.

Our world is in dire need of couples who boldly live out a joyfully imperfect bond. As stated, in the mid-1900s, Peter Marshall called matrimony "the highest halls of human happiness." Wouldn't it be wonderful if society again viewed marriage in this way?

For Michael Jordan, the cost of becoming the greatest player of all time was missing over nine thousand shots. For you and me, the price of a heroic marriage will be failing, getting back up, and trying again while continuing to celebrate all that is right in our union.

Marriage has a bad rap partly because partners hold onto unrealistic expectations.

Fairy tales tell us that after the ceremony, a couple is supposed to live happily ever after. Yet after the wedding challenges still exist. Three things you can count on are as follows:

1. You and your spouse will let each other down. After all, you were both imperfect before the wedding and will still be flawed after saying, "I do."
2. The two of you are going to rub each other the wrong way. If you were exactly alike, then one of you wouldn't be needed. Tension can be a good thing because it generates growth.
3. You and your spouse can celebrate amid the storm.

This last point is crucial. What if, instead of trying to attain perfection, you and your loved one embraced the beautiful mess? This strategy has certainly benefited Jenny and me. The two of us have not experienced a tidy year of life since we wed. A common phrase we use when problems arise is, "Of course, it's us! We should have known this wouldn't be easy."

As a blended family, Jenny and I have added stressors. The two of us are learning how to celebrate amidst the chaos and choose joy anyway. Appreciating this messy journey is our strategy day after day, and I certainly wouldn't want to live this adventure with anyone else!

So how are and your spouse celebrating success, failure, and everything in between? A heroic marriage isn't perfect. It's a union between two flawed individuals who incessantly choose joy.

Complete *The Heroic Marriage Challenge* by listing ten reasons to celebrate. Whether you and your spouse are living the dream or keep falling and getting back up, choose a heroic marriage — one defined by connection and joy!

The Heroic Marriage Challenge for Her

Choose a heroic marriage by celebrating all that is right in your bond. Complete today's challenge by finding ten reasons for joy. Bonus points for listing fifteen!

1. _____
2. _____
3. _____
4. _____
5. _____
6. _____
7. _____
8. _____
9. _____
10. _____
11. _____
12. _____
13. _____
14. _____
15. _____

The Heroic Marriage Challenge for Him

Choose a heroic marriage by celebrating all that is right in your bond. Complete today's challenge by finding ten reasons for joy. Bonus points for listing fifteen!

1. _____
2. _____
3. _____
4. _____
5. _____
6. _____
7. _____
8. _____
9. _____
10. _____
11. _____
12. _____
13. _____
14. _____
15. _____

Day 28:
Extreme Joy

Extreme sports are amazing! Growing up, I fell in love with running, hiking, snorkeling, mountain biking, and sky diving. Then, one day, while flipping through the television stations, I came across an extreme sports competition.

I was captivated by the breathtaking aerial stunts and technical skills that seemed to defy the possible. As someone who enjoys watching limits stretched, it's not surprising I once purchased a book entitled *14,000 Things to be Happy About*. As you might imagine, this isn't a book you read straight through. Instead, it's a compilation of 14,000 reasons for joy.

Author Barbara Kipfer tells how she began her list in the sixth grade. After the book's publication, she continued finding new reasons for happiness, and has now compiled over 145,000 reasons for joy.

Like an extreme mountain biker or skier, Barbara has taken gratitude to a new level. Dieter Uchtdorf said, "We can choose to be grateful no matter what," and according to Dietrich Bonhoeffer, "It is only with gratitude that life becomes rich." Uncommon gratitude is a common factor in the lives of successful men and women

This link between gratitude and success makes perfect sense. A lousy attitude requires no special talent. Anyone can complain, and most people do.

Gratitude, on the other hand, takes effort. Two years ago, I set out to compile my own gratitude list. I was posting weekly on my blog and challenged myself to write an article that contained 101 reasons for joy. This task was tougher than expected. Sure, it began easy enough. But around the midway point, I lost steam. By the time I reached number 101, I thought my bases were fully covered. Generating additional reasons for happiness seemed impossible.

Barbara's list proves I had not even scratched the surface. It has been said that most people are about as happy as they make up their minds to be, and I believe this is true.

What surprised me most is how ordinary Barbara's list is. Very few lines are mind-blowing. Instead, I find myself thinking, *Yes, I'm thankful for that and that and that too.* Barbara writes, "Paying attention to life — to its beauty, oddity, wonder — is what happiness is all about."[8] The genius of Barbara's book is its simplicity. Her ability to notice tiny pleasures allowed her to uncover a multitude of joy.

Likely, you and your loved one also have more reasons for joy than you realize. Joy is a common theme in this book, and although you already compiled a gratitude list, today's challenge is to take that list to the next level. I won't ask you to list 145,000 reasons for joy — or even 14,000. Similar to a muscle, joy grows with ongoing exertion.

In *The Extreme Joy Challenge*, list fifteen new reasons for joy. After all, there are many things going well in your marriage and your life, right? Your job is to find them.

The Extreme Joy Challenge for Her

Complete today's challenge by finding fifteen reasons for joy not included on a previous list.

1. _____
2. _____
3. _____
4. _____
5. _____
6. _____
7. _____
8. _____
9. _____
10. _____
11. _____
12. _____
13. _____
14. _____
15. _____

The Extreme Joy Challenge for Him

Complete today's challenge by finding fifteen reasons for joy not included on a previous list.

1. _____
2. _____
3. _____
4. _____
5. _____
6. _____
7. _____
8. _____
9. _____
10. _____
11. _____
12. _____
13. _____
14. _____
15. _____

Day 29:
Catching Foxes

In 2019, I had the honor of writing a brief excerpt in *Focus on the Family* magazine. I was asked to share one thing that helped Jenny and me have a happier relationship, and this is what I wrote:

"Ugh," I let out a sigh of frustration. Jenny's face dropped, and I could tell she was hurt. "I'm sorry, hon. That sigh wasn't about you. It's a bad habit that I am still trying to break." Jenny's face brightened as she graciously accepted my apology. My sighs are one of the many foxes that have invaded our marriage. Song of Solomon 2:15 tells how these tiny trespassers spoil the vines, making them a perfect metaphor for minute behaviors that generate strife.

My sighing habit began innocently enough. Deep breaths are a calming skill that I taught in a weekly class. Soon, I found myself practicing them at home. However, Jenny took them personally, as if I was sighing at her. Although I tried to explain, this did not improve our relationship. For nearly two weeks, our pattern was the same. I would sigh, Jenny would be hurt, and I would rationalize. Fortunately, I eventually caught on and decided to go foxhunting instead. I am learning that eliminating annoying habits is far better than trying to convince one's spouse to accept them. If irritating habits are causing tension in your marriage, then it may be time for you to go foxhunting too![9]

Since composing that article, I've learned the following about annoying behaviors:

- **Intentions matter little:** A repeat offense is still a repeat offense, whether we intended to harm or not.

- **Our loved one assigns the meaning:** People are meaning-making machines. In this case, Jenny made my sighs mean that I was frustrated with her. You and your loved one will assign significance to each other's actions. The meaning you assign may not be accurate, but you will determine what your loved one's actions mean to you.

- **Eliminating foxes is best:** Eliminating annoying habits out of love for our spouse is always best. The words *But honey, I didn't mean to offend you* are rarely helpful.

- **Connection is key:** Foxes are problems because they create distance between lovers. You and I cannot take a transgression back. Like toothpaste, once an offence is out, it is out for good. The bright side is we can apologize and reconnect fast.

The human brain views intimate connections as a survival need. They are just as important as air, water, food, and shelter. This is why foxes are such a big deal. When the bond with our spouse breaks, our brain goes haywire.

From my perspective, my sighs were just that — sighs. From Jenny's point of view, my deep breaths signaled disconnect, and this was devastating. Little foxes are dangerous because they wound our spouse more deeply than we realize.

Whether you call them foxes, annoying habits, or by any other name, it is best to eliminate these irritations. To complete *The Fox Hunting Challenge,* drive a pesky fox out of your relationship. Decide that when you blow it—as all couples do—you'll apologize, reconnect, and try again.

The Fox Hunting Challenge for Her

Describe a fox, or irritation in your relationship, that you need to eliminate

_____

_____

Brainstorm three ways you can reach out to your loved one when you mess up.

When I blow it and this fox sneaks back into our marriage, I will reach out to my loved one by:

    1. _____
    2. _____
    3. _____

When I reach for my loved one, I would like him to respond by _____

_____

_____

_____

_____

_____

_____

_____

The Fox Hunting Challenge for Him

Describe a fox, or irritation in your relationship, that you need to eliminate

_____

_____

Brainstorm three ways you can reach out to your loved one when you mess up.

When I blow it and this fox sneaks back into our marriage, I intend to reach out to my loved one by:

1. _____
2. _____
3. _____

When I reach for my loved one, I would like her to respond by _____

_____

_____

_____

_____

_____

_____

_____

Day 30:
The One Thing

The 1991 comedy *City Slickers* teased audiences with the secret to happiness. In this movie, Curly, a crusty cowboy, asks Mitch, the city slicker, "Do you know what the secret to happiness is? One thing, just one thing." When Mitch inquires, "What's the one thing?" Curly responds, "That's what you have to find out." Of course, the movie never reveals the secret.

Joyfully married couples also have a secret that boils down to one thing. Fortunately, this secret is not a tease. But before revealing the mystery, let's first examine what this one thing is not. When I ask couples how they know they are in love, I rarely hear answers like:

- We always get along.
- We communicate well.
- We have a good working relationship.
- We go on exotic vacations.

- We had a fancy wedding.
- Life together is easy.

Sure, some of these things are important, but none of them are essential. Couples tend to focus on these areas when their relationship is in turmoil. But they don't result in lasting joy unless they lead to the one thing. For example, lousy communication creates confusion, so learning how to communicate better is helpful. Yet few people get married solely because they communicate well.

When I ask couples how they know they are in love, typical answers include:

- We laugh a lot.
- We love spending time together.
- We remember the little things.
- We put each other's needs first.
- We share inside jokes.
- We look across the room and know what the other person is thinking.
- We talk about everything.
- We are totally honest with each other.

- We spend as much time together as possible.
- We are best friends.
- We support each other at all times.

The first list is characterized by a lack of problems and by grand acts of love. As far as I know, no heart was ever won with the words *You and I get along well. Let's marry.* And while gallant acts are nice, they are not enough to bind a couple's hearts together.

A joyful marriage is not about getting along nicely. Nor is it founded on one shining moment. In a joyful marriage, a couple's hearts unite through a habit of tenderhearted bonding.

The second list is summed up in the word *connection.* Each answer joyful couples gave describes a way their hearts intertwine. In marriage, a caring connection matters most. This is the one thing.

As stated in the introduction, a caring bond with our loved one enhances life in three ways: (1) It makes life's bright moments brighter, (2) it improves our physical health, including reducing the risk of heart attacks, and (3) it makes painful moments — both emotional and physical painful — hurt less.

Human beings are designed to connect. Over the last thirty-days, developing this type of joyful bond has been our goal. Hopefully, you and your loved one are more deeply rooted in love than ever before. If this is the case, then take time to celebrate, because the two of you exceed the norm.

Average couples live in quiet desperation, wondering when their pain will end. But joyfully married couples break out of the average by establishing daily moments of connection. As this book closes, how will you and your loved one continue to grow?

In *The Ongoing Connection Challenge,* create a vision for your future by brainstorming ways to keep growing your bond. I wish you happy connecting and a joyful marriage!

The Ongoing Connection Challenge for Her

Complete this final challenge by deciding how you will keep your connection habit going. List three small ways you will connect with your loved one daily. This can be as simple as a hug or a kiss or coffee together.

1. _____
2. _____
3. _____

Now, dream big and write down three larger ways you will connect over the next month. Get as specific as possible.

1. _____
2. _____
3. _____

Congratulations! You have completed *The Joyfully Married Challenge.* Now it's time to celebrate!

The Ongoing Connection Challenge for Him

Complete this final challenge by deciding how you will keep your connection habit going. List three small ways you will connect with your loved one daily. This can be as simple as a hug or a kiss or coffee together.

1. _____
2. _____
3. _____

Now, dream big and write down three larger ways you will connect over the next month. Get as specific as possible.

1. _____
2. _____
3. _____

Congratulations! You have completed *The Joyfully Married Challenge*. Now it's time to celebrate!

End Notes

1. Gottman, John, and Silver, Nan. *The Seven Principles for Making Marriage Work*. Three Rivers Press, 1999, p. 2.

2. Whitehead, Lorne. *"Domino 'chain reaction'."* American Journal of Physics 51, 04 June 1998.

3. Gottman, John, and Silver, Nan. *The Seven Principles for Making Marriage Work*. Three Rivers Press, 1999, p.48.

4. Hart, Archibald, and May, Sharon. *Safe Haven Marriage.* Thomas Nelson, 2003.

5. Chapman, Gary. The Five Love Languages. Northfield Publishing; Reprint Edition, 2015.

6. Jurchenko, Jed. This excerpt was first published in *Focus on the Family* magazine, June/July 2019.

7. Willink, Jocko, and Leif Babib. *Extreme Ownership, How U.S. Navy SEALs Lead and Win*. Pan Macmillan, 2018.

8. Kipfer, Barbara. *14,000 Things to Be Happy About*. Workman Publishing Company; Revised, Updated edition, October 2014.

9. Jurchenko, Jed. This excerpt was first published in *Focus on the Family* magazine, Dec 2018/Jan 2019.

Thumbs Up
or Thumbs Down

Thank you for purchasing this book!

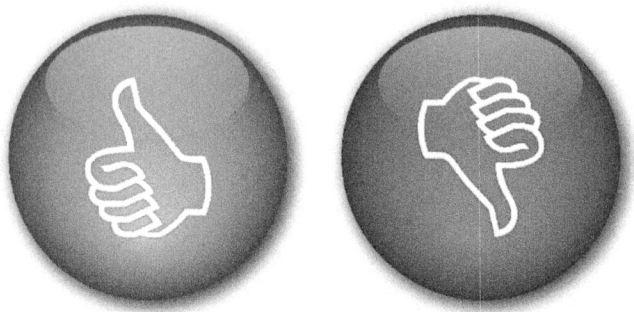

I would love to hear from you! Your feedback not only helps me grow as a writer but it also helps me to get books into the hands of those who need them most. Online reviews are one of the biggest ways that independent authors like me connect with new readers.

If you loved the book, could you please share your experience? Leaving feedback is as easy as answering any of these questions:

- What did you like about the book?

- What is your most important takeaway or insight?
- What have you done differently—or what will you do differently because of what you have read?
- Whom would you recommend this book to?

Of course, I am looking for honest reviews. So if you have a minute to share your experience, good or bad, please consider leaving a review!

I look forward to hearing from you!

Sincerely, Jed Jurchenko

About the Author

Jed Jurchenko is a husband, a father to four girls, and a foster-father to two more. He is also a psychology professor, therapist, and coach. Jed helps busy couples, families, and entrepreneurs grow their relationships by focusing their attention on the ones who matter most.

Jed graduated from Southern California Seminary with a Master of Divinity and returned to complete a second master's degree in psychology. In their free time, Jed and Jenny enjoy walking on the beach, reading, and spending time together as a family.

Continue the Conversation

If you enjoyed this book, I would love it if you would leave a review on Amazon. Your feedback is a huge encouragement to me as an emerging author and helps books like this one get noticed. It only takes a minute, and every review is greatly appreciated. Oh—and please feel free to stay in touch too!

Email: jed@coffeeshopconversations.com

Twitter: @jjurchenko

Facebook: Coffee Shop Conversations

More Creative Conversations

This book and other creative conversation starters are available at www.Amazon.com.

Take your relationship from bland to inspired, passionate, and connected as you grow your insights into your spouse's inner world! Whether you are newly dating or nearing your golden anniversary, these questions are for you! This book will help you share your heart and dive into your partner's inner world.

131 Creative Conversations for Couples

More Creative Conversations

These creative conversation starters will inspire your kids to pause their electronics, grow their social skills, and develop lifelong relationships!

This book is for children and tweens who desire to build face-to-face connections and for everyone who wants to help their kids connect in an increasingly disconnected world. Get your kids talking with this activity book the entire family will enjoy.

131 Conversations That Engage Kids

Made in the USA
Las Vegas, NV
16 February 2022

44016796R00115